The
SHARPEST
Soft Skill

10 Proven Etiquette Strategies for Business Success

Maryanne Parker

Editors:
Beth Riley
Marilyn Tenney

ISBN-13: 978-1534830080
ISBN-10: 1534830081

In loving Memory of my Beloved Mother

This book is dedicated to you, the reader!

I tell my students, "When you get these jobs that you have been so brilliantly trained for, just remember that your real job is that if you are free, you need to free somebody else. If you have some power, then your job is to empower somebody else. This is not just a grab-bag candy game."

—Toni Morrison

Dear reader,

Let me introduce myself, welcome you into my world, and share with you how this book was born. We all have our own unique life story—one which defines us, determines our future, and makes us or breaks us. Just like many other single moms in the world, I could easily have become just a statistic. I didn't allow that to happen, though: if I had, my voice wouldn't be heard, and I wouldn't be able to help anybody. My kids told me I have so many stories to tell that I should write a book, so here I am, writing this for you. Now that I'm fully equipped, emotionally and psychologically, to share my story and message, I hope that this book will help *you* to dream big, fight hard for your happiness, execute your vision, and write your own success story that has a positive impact on your world, your community, and society as a whole. We all have something to share, and we can all learn from each other as long as we're ready and willing to really listen to each other.

When I first came to the United States a decade ago, I was a happily married young woman, full of faith, energy, positivity, and hope for an amazing, promising future in the greatest country in the world. My daughter was one year old, and I was expecting my son to arrive shortly. I never imagined that anything could go wrong and spoil all this happiness. Everything was perfect, just like a beautiful, romantic movie, until my life turned upside down.

Due to very unfortunate circumstances, shortly after my arrival, I found myself homeless, with an infant and a toddler, living in a shelter for victims of domestic violence on the central coast of California. My beautiful, radiant dream had turned into an ugly nightmare, and I was the reluctant main character. Unfortunately, I wasn't dreaming—it was actually my story. I was in shock. Everything in my world was broken: my life, my love, my marriage, my heart, and even myself—I was literally broke. I asked myself, "Is it really as bad as it looks?" The answer was "Yes, it really *is* that bad. Actually, it's worse than what it looks." Imagine yourself, newly arrived in a foreign country, with two young kids. You don't have any family here, you don't know anyone, you're living in a shelter in a city you'd never heard of before, and you're completely broke.

That was my reality at the time. I had two choices: I

could give up or try to turn the tables around. The latter option didn't look like much of a possibility at the time, but I definitely knew I couldn't give up—that just wasn't me. I had my kids to care for, and I had to find a way to build a dignified life for them as well as myself. I couldn't afford to be depressed, because I had a long way to go. I knew I couldn't get distracted, and I had to fight, because, as we all know, life happens, and many times it happens in a way we do not expect at all!

I received marvelous counseling and guidance from professionals who specialize in dealing with cases such as mine. I moved to the finest city in America, San Diego, California—one of the most beautiful places I have ever seen, as well as one of the most expensive. I joined an amazing organization called Dress for Success San Diego, which supports underprivileged women like I was at the time, and my life started to turn around little by little. I started working and kept pushing forward, and I met some great people. Piece by piece, I began to create the life I had always wanted. I was on a mission to build a great life for my kids.

Five years later, I purchased my own house in San Diego. It wasn't my dream house, but it was *mine*. The house was run-down and wasn't in a very attractive area, but the real estate broker told me, "Listen, if you have a vision, you can win big if you purchase this property. Many people have seen it, and they didn't like it because it doesn't look attractive, but you can make it happen. I think this could be great for you and your kids." I wasn't really concerned about the potential at the time; all I knew was that I wanted to have a yard with space for the kids to play, and I didn't want to be moving every year from apartment to apartment. Some of my friends advised me not to buy the house. I knew they meant well, but I had to do what I had to do. When the broker told me, "This property was last sold for almost $550,000. You'll be getting it for a fraction of this amount," all I could do was wonder who had paid so much money for this swamp! I couldn't even comprehend that amount—I was a divorced, single mom from Bulgaria, so it was a huge sum for me. Still, I purchased the property at just the right time, and it turned out to be a wonderful investment. Just five years later, market prices went up like crazy and my equity skyrocketed. I even read in the *New York Times* that the area I had moved into just a few years earlier was now "living a new Renaissance," and many wealthy people were moving to downtown San Diego from Rancho Santa Fe! Are you kidding me? I was amazed at how crazy life could be! So that was how I began my real estate adventure without even knowing anything about real estate.

Blessings continued to pour into my life after all the drama I had gone through. I opened my own business, Manor of Manners. I started writing articles, conducting seminars, and taking on public speaking engagement. I became a spokesperson for Dress for Success San Diego. I travel all over the world, learning about other cultures and incorporating anything and everything I learn into my classes, articles, and gatherings with my friends.

The most important lessons I've learned in my time in the United States are to work hard and to care about and contribute to my community. I have received so much generosity and met so many good-hearted people—something I'd never experienced before in my life. That's why I know I live in the greatest country in the world. I am definitely living the American dream! The way I was able to accomplish all this was because of my sensitivity and knowledge of etiquette. I was able to work and become friends with high-profile international dignitaries, and all of my success is based on my knowledge and use of soft skills.

I have a BA degree in Accounting and Financial Control from Sofia, Bulgaria, as well as the many "hard skills" necessary to work in the corporate world, but my competitive edge was in the way I applied soft skills everywhere I went and worked. That's why I'm sharing this information with you: if I can achieve success—writing a book, starting my own business, traveling the world, having amazing friends and a great support system—after moving to a foreign country with two kids and having to learn a foreign language, then you can do it, too!

Besides the etiquette strategies I'll share with you, I would like to also offer a few important reminders for your success:

1. Follow your instincts—sometimes people mean well, but they do not live *your* life.
2. Jump—don't analyze too much. Just do it! Playing it safe will keep you just that: safe. If you want to make progress, you'll have to jump when things are a little scary and uncertain.
3. Sometimes being broke can be a blessing—use it! You won't stay broke forever, and if you're reading this book, you obviously want to learn something that someone else can teach you and set out on your road to success.

Now, because this book is not about me, I want to dive right into the etiquette strategies that helped me get and keep a job (even during the recent recession, when everybody was losing their jobs), get promoted, build incredible relationships, and manage to build a strong support system. The ideas in this book are not complicated at all. Tony Robbins (one of the most successful business strategists in history) says, "Complexity is the enemy of execution." We are all interested in the end result, and in this book I'll give you the main elements which helped me succeed, instead of becoming another sad statistic.

Finally, I can't wait to read your own stories and learn from you. Good luck to you, my dearest friends! Please keep me posted on your journeys to success!

Table of Contents

Introduction

Welcome!

I applaud your desire to learn about business etiquette in the modern-day business world. With more than a billion meetings of every type (in-person and virtual) held every year, it's more important than ever to have the skills that will help you interact well with people from all across the globe who come from widely varying cultures and walks of life.

According to research conducted at Stanford University, 85 percent of business success is based on our soft skills. It's not an isolated situation when great business owners can't retain clients because their employees lack customer service skills or poor manners cause distractions at the office. We all need to remember that common sense is not always common practice, and it needs to be reinforced on a daily basis. This book can be very helpful to your future business success, and all the tactics you'll find here are proven to be effective and applicable to real situations. Go now, and reach for your full potential!

Why etiquette?

Many people think of etiquette as a "fluffy," outdated subject. It's often associated with ballroom dancing and outrageous, odd rules that are hardly applicable to modern life. Some people don't even know what etiquette is. After you finish reading this book, you'll realize not only that etiquette is *the* "sharpest" soft skill in the twenty-first century, but also that it's used in every social and business situation. Etiquette is a timeless practice; its purpose is simply to show respect and make everyone feel valued, comfortable, and at ease. Good manners enabled me to be extremely successful in corporate America, and that is the inspiration behind my etiquette consulting business, Manor of Manners. Etiquette expert Jeanne Nelson said it quite well: "A degree will get your foot in the door; good manners will open it." In the United States, we refer to good manners as good business and place a lot of importance on soft skills as a management tool. Honing soft skills is a crucial element of achieving professional success.

History of etiquette

Louis XIV of France (also known as "The Sun King"), who reigned from May 14, 1643 to September 1, 1715, is perceived as one of the most powerful and successful monarchs in history. France became the major European power and changed incredibly during his regime, transforming from a country with primitive, medieval practices into a sophisticated, refined, and polished nation. We associate French wine, perfumes, cheese, champagne, and almost everything exquisitely French with the Sun King.

Louis XIV loved to host lavish celebrations and parties at his famous Palace of Versailles. Unfortunately, though, the palace's premises were in terrible shape after each of these royal gatherings. Nobles jumped into the fountains (especially during the summer), stomped his grass, didn't walk in the designated areas, picked the meticulously maintained flowers in his perfect gardens, and littered everywhere. The king was known as a man of rules and tidiness, so after consulting with his gardeners, he created many little signs to place around the palace grounds that would address these issues: "Do not pick the flowers," "Do not stomp the grass," "Do not jump into the fountains," and many more. These had a tremendous effect, and thus the seeds of etiquette were planted.

Louis XIV also used etiquette in a very sophisticated way to control his court. He created so many rules for dress, ballroom dancing, and table manners that the nobles were too busy learning etiquette and mannerisms to organize internal revolutions. Some of the rules seem extremely strange to us in these modern times, but they were highly popular during his reign. Many nobles went into debt because they had to purchase expensive, modern (for the time) attire, which was also a passive method of internal control. This was the beginning of the power of the sharpest soft skill—etiquette: from Louis XIV to modern manners.

CHAPTER ONE

Hard Skills vs Soft Skills

We all know that there's a big difference between hard and soft skills. In order to recognize their importance, we should be very much aware of them. Hard skills are the skills we learn in school, college, and at work. They usually require mastery (like every other skill) without any emotional involvement. These are the skills we usually associate with IQ. A high IQ is impressive and might play a large part in your success, but no matter what kind of job you have, you will have to develop and possess at least some soft skills. The soft skills I've had to work on throughout my professional career include: communication (verbal and nonverbal); resourcefulness; problem-solving; handling constructive criticism; attentiveness; collaborating instead of competing with others (especially in an office environment where, on many occasions, we need to work well in teams); dependability; emotional intelligence; and many more.

When I first arrived in the United States, I had to find a job as soon as possible. I didn't know what to expect or where to start. I knew that I was presenting myself well, and my resume was picked immediately from hundreds of others. However, after I got the job, for some reason I couldn't keep it. This happened probably three times in one year. I was extremely disappointed and hurt. At the same time, I was desperate because I had to provide a decent living for my children. I'm just talking about a regular living, not a lavish lifestyle, but I couldn't even achieve that. I was a skilled professional, using all the hard skills necessary to do well in my corporate field. What was I doing wrong?

I wanted to be brutally honest with myself because you can blame people for your failures only so much; it depends on how far you want to go in life. After dissecting my behavior, mannerisms, communication patterns, and many other elements of the soft skills palette, I realized that I had a few weaknesses: I'm extremely introverted, not a great communicator, not focused enough, and—worst of all—I'm a very bad listener. I guess all this had to do with the personal problems I was still recovering from.

I resolved to work hard on my soft skills, and I got so good at it that I would go for a job interview just to prove to myself how much I had improved (which at times was really fascinating). After two years of self-assessment, developing the best strategies to deal with people, and most importantly, finding the way to work in harmony and contribute to everybody's success, I felt I had really accomplished something. Of course, every time I went for an interview, I answered the job-related questions well, but I also knew how to present myself in a way that allowed me to not only *get* the job but also to *retain* the job.

Here's a great example. I started a new job during the recent recession, and to my surprise, when a high percentage of the company's people were laid off, they kept me! I asked my boss why they decided to keep me. The answer: because my customer service skills, loyalty, and professional ethics were exceptional! Remember, I have a degree in accounting, so I wasn't a receptionist or a front desk representative, but yes, I had to deal with many customers, vendors, and other outside people, so I guess I had become the face of the company in a way. I stayed with that company for years, but things happen, and we need to move up or move on.

Even though a degree is important, I've only been asked to present my degree once in my entire corporate career, and that was because I was being promoted to a higher position, along with a change of management. This happened after I had worked for the company for five years. In other words, you get a job based on your presentation. Your soft skills will help get you hired and keep the job!

I'm sure you understand that the same concept applies in regards to working with business partners. We are all human beings who are influenced by the same basic principles, although some of us much more easily than others. Right now, I'd like you to try an exercise. Write down five soft skills you would like to work on improving over the next three months. Also, write down the achievements or goals you would like to accomplish, and keep a consistent attitude. After those three months, you can decide to develop three more: educate yourself, practice, and apply. The important thing is that you need to be honest with yourself.

The more you're aware of your weak points, the better.

DATE:	SOFT SKILL:	DESIRED END RESULT:
1.		
2.		
3.		
4.		
5.		

Always remember that everything works as a package. Just wearing perfect office attire won't get and help you retain the job. It takes much more than that. Remind yourself that just because some of your skills need improvement, that doesn't mean you don't already have some incredible people skills—you just want to be better! This will help you to be more accomplished, that's all. As I said before, it's great to have a high IQ, but if it's not combined with an equally high EQ (Emotional Intelligence Quotient), the result won't be that great, and you won't be able to achieve your full potential.

CHAPTER TWO

Emotional Intelligence

Since I was a teenager, I've been fascinated by the topic of emotional intelligence (also called emotional quotient, or EQ). I recognized very early the differences in people and how they react in certain situations. I realized, even at a young age, that some people have this high level of "sensitivity"—what *Psychology Today* calls "Emotional awareness, including the ability to identify your own emotions and those of others." (See https://www.psychologytoday.com/basics/emotionalintelligence.) Many times, we refer to the way we act simply as common sense, but as we know, common sense is not that common, and it's easy to see that EQ is not actually a common practice. What is Emotional Intelligence? We've all heard that high EQ, and not just the level of your IQ, is the key factor that opens doors to success. I agree completely: many people have impressive degrees without a high level of EQ, but unfortunately, they probably drive taxis for a living (or more likely, for survival) while some people—like Tony Robbins, who is one of the most influential business strategists of all time and runs, a multibillion-dollar business—don't have traditional degrees, but they have PhDs in results.

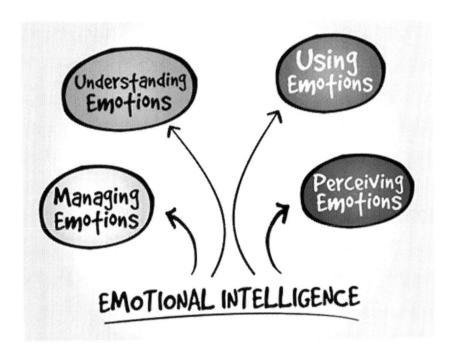

FOUR COMPONENTS OF EQ:

1. Self-awareness—you need to be able to challenge yourself to get the results you want to achieve. There's a reason why self-awareness is one of the most crucial elements, not just for a professional career and business success, but for personal success as well. Without self-awareness, we can't reach our full potential, because in many cases we'll assume that we know how to react in a certain situation,

only to find that our reaction wasn't the correct one. Self-awareness comes from personal experience and analyzing what works or doesn't work well in a variety of different situations. We need to train ourselves to pay attention to details. To be able to communicate with others, you need to know who you really are, and this won't happen overnight. Just be patient; learn as much as you can about yourself on a daily basis, and you'll be ready soon enough. When you know your reactions, you'll be able to be in control of most of the situations in your life.

2. Self-management—"A moment of patience in a moment of anger saves you a hundred moments of regrets." Take control of your emotions, don't lose patience, don't react angrily, and don't be vindictive about situations. In many cases, when strong emotions are involved and you can avoid certain relationships, it's probably best to do so. If you can't, self-management is the only option. I won't sugarcoat it; this is not an easy task. Many people lose control, which can lead to disaster. Let's face it: many people are much ruder than they should be, and it's usually because they have no idea how to behave in social situations. They often have a complex based on prior experiences, and this is their defense mechanism. In many cases, they might try to provoke you because they are used to being "attacked" or provoked. We all experience this every single day: while we're driving on the freeway, shopping at the store, working in the office, and just

about anywhere else. People have different levels of mannerisms, and unfortunately, because we don't live on an island, we have to deal with that, and we need to really control situations so we don't fall into their traps. This leads to point #3.

3. Social awareness—this is your exposure to the world around you. Learn, educate yourself, and collect as many different experiences as you can. It's always good to be positive about life. We need to be aware that we all have different backgrounds, understandings, and knowledge. We have to realize that people have different levels of responsibility and varying degrees of their "very best." We need to know how to handle even the most annoying situations, and this is where life becomes interesting: knowing how to react in the best way possible. If someone behaves in what you think is a strange or rude manner, try to look for something positive, or turn the tables around and simply respond with a nice, polite answer. Just try not to be sarcastic—that will only increase the negativity.

4. Relationship management—get excited about people! Meet them with purpose: build them up, help them, become genuinely interested in them, and influence them in a positive way. I've built a lot of wonderful, solid relationships that will last for years to come simply because I'm curious, intrigued, and sincerely interested in learning about new people. Of course, you'll need to take good care of your "old" relationships with people as well. You need to be authentic. Don't get involved with people just be-

cause you think you may gain something; at the end of the day, you'll only lose. People are sensitive and careful about whom they open up to. Everything is based on trust, mutual respect, and understanding. Be a person with integrity. Always try to give more than you receive. This is much more enriching, justifying, and fulfilling.

Are we born with this "sensitivity" called emotional intelligence? This question used to fascinate me a lot, even though I had a basic idea of what the answer was. I personally think we are born with it, but I also believe that a certain level of emotional intelligence can be developed and reinforced. Let's face it; it's crucial to have the ability to communicate in a proper way and to socialize with people.

I frequently incorporate lessons about emotional intelligence when I teach etiquette. Modern-day etiquette doesn't necessarily involve ballroom dancing and white gloves, but it does require the ability to be civil and make other people feel at ease. Thus, there is a very strong connection between emotional intelligence and etiquette. They can both be learned and serve you with the same success. Components of emotional intelligence carry over quite well when you're discussing etiquette:

1. Perceiving emotions—body language and facial expressions. If you learn enough about these components, you'll be able to decode some important characteristics that might help you decided if a person is

someone you might be willing to work with, do business with, or even develop a friendship with. Some people will be truthful, some people won't, and you'll be able to detect that. A degree in economics or in orbital engineering won't help you in this regard, but emotional intelligence definitely will! Be mindful of the fact that many situations are predetermined from the very beginning. We may even see certain signs but consciously refuse to recognize them, or we might not be confident enough to trust our emotional intelligence.

2. Using your emotions to prioritize properly—to have your priorities in order is an essential part of your success. If you always do what you like instead of what you should, you will often find yourself in an extremely unfavorable position. If you want to progress in life and eventually do what you really want to do, you usually have to start with subjects or tasks you don't really like but that are the most important at the time. When you start feeling too comfortable, that's a sign that you need to stretch yourself and move on to the next task. We all need to prioritize at one moment or another. Just like executives have to use the proper judgment to lead their companies, we as individuals make executive decisions on a daily basis in our own lives. If we don't prioritize well, we can end up in difficult situations.

3. Understanding emotions—being polite and well-mannered, along with relating to other people's emotions, is a crucial element of success. You need

to use your sensitivity and try to be sympathetic; if you do, then you'll be perceived much more favorably than someone who ignores people's emotions. Of course, we shouldn't do this just for our own benefit; trying to understand people's emotions is a noble skill.

I'm sure we all know people who are very critical and judgmental. At times, this can be extremely annoying. Remember the saying, "Before you criticize a man, walk a mile in his shoes"? The main lesson in this adage is to try to understand the other person's feelings or the reasons behind why they do certain things. In many situations, because of a lack of exposure or just plain ignorance, some people simply won't be able to accept or understand other people. The fact someone doesn't think or behave like you is not an excuse for unreasonable judgment. Showing empathy requires the desire to understand the person in front of you. It doesn't require personal involvement or shared experience. It only involves the desire to show compassion and understanding.

4. The ability to manage emotions effectively—with class and grace. Many times, the way you manage your emotions will be the critical component of how you handle everything in general. You need to be composed, classy, and poised, no matter what. Of course, if you know what triggers negative emotions in you, you'll be better prepared to control them. Showing class and professionalism elevates you above the circumstances. Have you ever been in a

situation that, looking back, you wish you had handled better than you did? This is what you seek to avoid. By learning to manage your emotions well, you'll reduce those badly handled and embarrassing moments in your life.

Possessing emotional intelligence doesn't change the amount of effort that's required. Sometimes being aware of the fact that you have a high level of emotional intelligence can hold you back in a way because you might be confident that you can still get ahead without putting in much work. This is far from the truth. The secret is to combine your EQ with hard work, and then you will be unstoppable! After you recognize the power of emotional intelligence, you can start utilizing it as an important technique in all of your interpersonal interactions. If you weren't born with this particular skill, you can develop it. We commit to developing all kinds of skills when we have the desire to improve our lives.

CHAPTER THREE

Not Everyone is Our Client, and That's Okay

After we gain confidence through success (and *every* achievement, large or small, is a step toward success), we need to realize that not everyone is our client, and that's perfectly fine. We can't work for every company, and that's okay, too. Just because you go for an interview with a company doesn't mean that's be the company you should work for. You're going there to interview *them* as well. If they don't call you for a second interview, that might be a good thing—it will take you closer to where you *should* be working.

Being a successful entrepreneur and small business owner requires a lot of communication, observation, and relationship building. You should start using your knowledge of etiquette to help you form and maintain those strong business relationships. Business relationships are just like personal relationships: you usually know from the very beginning whether they will work out. If you're like most people, you often follow your instincts to determine the people you like to work and socialize with. Believe me, the way a person interviews you will tell you a lot about their level of professionalism. It's another thing entirely if you choose to ignore the red flags for whatever reason, but if you follow the simple, basic etiquette practices below that you can apply right away, you'll enjoy a greater sense of satisfaction and success, both in your business and personal relationships.

1. Emails—a response to an email shouldn't take more than forty-eight hours. If someone takes a few days to respond, he or she should offer you a really good explanation. Of course, sometimes correspondence can get lost, so if you don't receive a response to your first email, send a second one. If the response is vague or you don't sense any energy or enthusiasm, it's probably not a good idea to collaborate with them.

When you receive the response, you can sense the level of the person's professionalism from the grammar, wording, and tone of the email. Some people start with "Dear Maryanne," and some simply say "Hi, Maryanne." They might call you by your first name, or they may use the more formal Mr. or Ms.

It is *never* ok to use all capital letters in text. In the twenty-first century, everyone should know that, but believe it or not, a lot of people still use all capital letters. Don't be one of them! All caps are annoying and unprofessional.

One other very important thing: do *not* write long emails. This is another indicator of professionalism and consideration. Nobody has time to read long emails. Make it easy for the recipient to get right to the heart of what you're trying to communicate. Write about the essence of the situation, issue, target, or project. Use bullet points if you need to. We'll talk more about this in Chapter 6.

2. Phone calls—returning calls is exceptionally important. When you call and leave a message, you have a right to expect the person to return your call. If people take longer than usual to return your calls, they're probably not well organized, and their business practices are likely missing a sense of balance. I wouldn't work with a person who can't return my calls, takes a week to get back to me or—worse yet—doesn't get back to me at all but still wants me to collaborate on a project with them.

Sometimes people will leave a message at a time when they know that you're long gone for the day. In a way, this could be perceived as good because they've at least returned the call, but it still depends on the situation. If they indicate they'll return the call the next day at their first opportunity, this is a very good sign; it shows responsibility and professionalism.

You need to have a system to track phone calls. When you get a call, write it down on a piece of paper or a notebook. When you return the call, cross it off your list. A good practice is to start with the oldest phone call first.

Some people seem to think you don't have anything else to do and that you should always be on standby just in case they need you. This should *never* be the case. Your time is just as valuable as anyone else's. At the same time, though, you usually can't change the mindset of those types of people. You can simply withdraw yourself and your business from these situations.

Sometimes hiring and/or collaborating with the wrong people can cost you thousands of dollars. You need to be very vigilant, because the way people do *anything* is the way they do *everything*. They won't be able to hide every sign that they aren't capable of doing certain things. They might even misrepresent themselves unintentionally just because they've been doing it for so long that it's become the norm for them. Many times you may even wonder how they stay in business, and guess what? Only 4 percent of businesses survive past the ten-year mark, and surviving doesn't mean succeeding—it simply means that they're keeping their head above water. That's all. Do you really want these types of people to be your collaborators and business partners?

3. Being late for a meeting—this is a very serious indication that there is a missing organizational element. Don't get me wrong; things happen to all of us—we forget our keys, get into an accident, the babysitter doesn't show up on time—but if you hear people say they've been trying to work on the issue of being late for a long time and they're still always late, that's a sign that they won't be a good fit for your business's success. No matter how insignificant you may feel or how important they may be in everybody else's eyes, this lack of simple courtesy is a sure sign that you won't be able to develop a mutually beneficial relationship.

    One time when I went for an interview with a company, the person who interviewed me was forty minutes late. Is this a good sign? What do you think? It means that this person either forgot about the interview or thought I was so desperate that I would stay until they arrived. This shows that they have no respect for the other person. After this, they called to inform me that I was hired (which, as I told you earlier, was not unusual because I know how to use my knowledge and application of soft skills to get hired. Besides, I was writing this book, and I wanted to make you aware of certain office behaviors and share it with friends like you.) They asked me if I could start on a particular date. A few days before my start date, the HR manager called to ask if I could start on a different date because there was no one to train me on the original start date. I'm not making any of this up. Does this sound like a professional company to you? Exactly! That's my point!

4. Appearance—it may seem like common sense, but people who are unkempt, sloppy, and unclean won't be your best bet either. If they don't have the desire to take care of themselves, it means they'll probably be sloppy in their business relationships as well. Besides, we like to work with pleasant people around us. The people we do collaborate with represent our image and brand as well. I'm sure you have heard the saying that we are perceived by association, and we build our image based on that, too.

5. Respectful demeanor—people who try to intimidate you, who are dishonest, or who react with jealousy and insecurity because they sense your drive and commitment to success won't be good business partners. We live and build our dreams in the twenty-first century on a very different platform, where everything is based on collaboration. Those ancient cutthroat, competitive ways are, thankfully, long gone. If people don't give you the respect you deserve, move on. You'll find plenty of others who will.

CHAPTER FOUR

Cultural Diversity and How to Maintain Great Rapport

Cultural Diversity and How to Maintain Great Rapport

CULTURAL AWARENESS

According to etiquette rules from a bygone era, we should avoid certain subjects like religion, politics, and money because we're all so different. In the twenty-first century, though, interacting with people from varied cultural backgrounds and beliefs is simply the norm. This can only be a positive thing because we learn so much more from our differences than from our similarities. We live and work in a global environment, and it's necessary to be exposed to diversity in every way if we want to have a pleasant, productive, and successful life. The following rules will help you learn how to communicate confidently with people of different cultures and faiths.

Six Interfaith Etiquette Rules

1. Learn about the other person's religion. In most cases, if it's explained well, it will make sense. Share as much information as you can about your religion, too. Religious people or people with a high level of spirituality are usually pretty tolerant of other faiths and beliefs (of course, there are always extreme cases). We don't want to include everybody in the same category. Many spiritual people learn about different religions because they want to have greater knowledge and, in general, they like to be informed about the differences and the similarities. In a particular conversation, if you do disagree with something and you need more evidence, you always can ask the individual you are speaking with what source he is using. And you always can do your own research. Most of the time, truth emerges through engaging in genuine, respectful conversation.

2. Explore. It's a very good idea to explore other people's religions. Visit their church, temple, synagogue, or mosque. Even fasting for a couple of days can help you to experience the feeling and start to form a bond of shared values. Explore by traveling, reading books on the topic, and associating with people who have different beliefs.

3. Be respectful during their observations, prayers, or other religious practices. For example, one of my friends was observing Ramadan (I am a Christian), so my respect for her led me to refrain from eating or drinking around her or her family during the observation of their holy month. In response, she told me that I didn't have to refrain from eating because *she* rejoices when I *do* eat during the day. In other words, we were both trying to show respect for each other in our own ways. We didn't judge each other or show any disrespect regarding our religions; we were both trying to create a pleasant environment for everybody around us.

4. Always look for similarities. You'll be surprised how many positive ideas other seemingly different religions share with your own. The differences will be always there, but that just makes life more enjoyable. If you do have a certain viewpoint regarding a topic or you disagree with a person about something, you should be confident in your source, and you need to be familiar with the topic. Don't just talk, argue, or look for conflict. Can the topic of religion only be based on the holy books you're referring to?

5. Don't be provocative, especially with your questions, clothing, food, or drink. For example, shorts and showing a lot of cleavage could be pretty disrespectful to devoutly religious people. Also, don't drink alcohol or bring it as a gift during religious holidays if you aren't sure about how others might react. More often than not, in some cultures, it will be seen as an offense or a sign of disrespect, and you might not be invited a second time to join their gathering, party, or event.

6. If a conversation or situation gets really uncomfortable, just leave it. In many cases, this happens only if people start digging deeper and deeper, looking for a conflict, or they become too pushy and try to convince you that their religion is better than yours. An argument is only possible if more than one person is involved, so be the "adult." Sometimes it isn't easy, but it will be worth it in the long run. Don't always try to have the last word or tell people that you obviously can't agree with them on the topic.

We are in a global workplace, and these etiquette rules could be very useful if we try to utilize them as much as we can.

CHAPTER FIVE

Punctuality

In some countries, punctuality is not considered an essential element of professionalism, but in the United States, this is one of the most important components of a successful business. In the U.S., time is money, so being on time shows your dedication to your job, your business partners, and your clients. It also shows that you are capable of handling responsibilities. Let's face it; who wants to work with a person who doesn't project the most basic sense of commitment?

Have you ever wondered why Americans are so time-minded? The reason lies in America's DNA. Back in the day, during the time of land grabs and the Gold Rush, people knew if they weren't one of the first, they'd be one of the last. It was the "first-come, first-served" philosophy. If you weren't "on time," what could have been yours would be taken by someone else. This concept has carried on as part of the American psyche for many generations. As modern Americans, we often can't justify this time-driven mentality, but we follow it anyway. It can be both a curse and a blessing: always wanting to be on time can sometimes keep you in chains, but on another note, you can usually get more done in a specified space of time than someone who lacks a sense of punctuality. Time is something you can't recover or purchase.

What does punctuality actually say about you? It says that you respect the other person and their time, that you respect yourself as well, that you manage your time efficiently, and that you are disciplined, reliable, and trustworthy. Well-organized people will get to the meeting, no matter the circumstances. Being there on time builds a strong reputation. Of course, in the event of those inevitable situations beyond your control, you'll be able to excuse yourself in a reasonable manner.

I remember a time when I was working with a client from the Middle East, where punctuality is not exactly the strongest asset people possess. I was always, *always* on time for our classes, and when we talked about future projects, he felt very confident in introducing me to other people as a very punctual person. I didn't know that he was paying attention to it, but for me this skill was so well developed that it was already second nature. If you can train yourself to be punctual, you will reduce your stress and add greater quality to your life.

On a scale of one to ten, how do you rate yourself when it comes to punctuality? Do you need to work on this feature? Here's a simple five-step program which is guaranteed to improve your punctuality.

1. For one week, try to be ten minutes early for every meeting. If getting ready for work on time is challenging, prepare everything you need for the next day the night before so you don't have to focus on anything in the morning except that you need to arrive to your destination ten minutes earlier. Decide exactly what you'll wear the next day and prepare your clothes the night before (including ironing). Try it on; if there are stains, a damaged zipper, or a missing button, you don't want to be dealing with this in the morning. Get your shoes ready, too; if they need polishing, don't wait 'til the morning. If you are going to take your lunch from home, get it ready the night before. Make sure you have gas in your car. These are just a few examples of what you should do to prevent the kinds of avoidable situations which constantly make you late.

2. Go to bed thirty minutes earlier than usual. You'll be better rested, and you won't need an additional ten minutes (which can easily turn into thirty) to wake up after your alarm goes off. Lack of sleep decreases your productivity, anyway, so it's a no-brainer.

3. Never talk down to yourself because you're the person who's always late. Being late is an unhealthy habit, and you have the power to change it. And you will! It is always up to *you* to create your winning rituals.

4. Talk to your family about it and ask for their support in helping you be more punctual. They shouldn't be the ones who make you late. If they don't understand the importance, then they're not exactly your biggest cheerleaders, and that's okay, but it never hurts to try.

5. Don't overschedule your calendar. You are only human, and you can only be in one place at a time.

I know these five techniques are effective because they worked for me. I had to train myself to be organized and punctual, not because of the culture around me, but because I had a lot of things to accomplish in a very tight time frame. Besides, I felt that I was running out of time and I didn't really want to miss out on life because my organizational skills were so poor.

CHAPTER SIX

Communication Skills and Introductions

> *" I've learned that people will forget what you said,*
> *people will forget what you did,*
> *but people will never forget how you made them feel. "*

—Maya Angelou

Communication is one of the most important skills you will use as a business professional. Your nonverbal communication skills need to convey a positive, professional, warm approach, because a client or business acquaintance might not remember your name, but they most assuredly will remember how you make them feel.

Your verbal skills need to meet the necessary criteria for a business professional. Use polite words; don't use slang, curse words, or bad language. While slang and the occasional curse word can give the illusion that you are relaxed, it often makes others uncomfortable and shows poor vocabulary skills.

NONVERBAL COMMUNICATION

Let's talk first about some of the most important non-verbal communication techniques that are crucial for business success. Elements like body language are extremely important when it comes to influencing business colleagues and clients. This doesn't mean we should try to manipulate people, but by applying nonverbal techniques appropriately, we can position ourselves in the most positive way.

Eye Contact

When you meet new people and want to introduce yourself in a way that's memorable, eye contact is extremely important. (In Western culture, eye contact is a requirement, but it might not be applicable for other cultures in similar situations. Make yourself aware of those differences.)

We should always make eye contact when we meet people and introduce ourselves, but it can backfire if it's not done properly. What does that mean? Appropriate eye contact is just that—we don't stare at the other person's eyes in an intrusive way because we might be perceived as aggressive, dominant, controlling, and at times even vulgar and inappropriate. I always tell my young students that they should actually try to recognize the eye color of person they're meeting (which takes just a few seconds), then move their eyes away from the person's face.

If, for whatever reason, you don't feel comfortable making full eye contact, look at just one of the other person's eyes or even the bridge of the nose. Sometimes it can be more comfortable to focus on the space between the other person's eyes. Eye contact might look easy for some people to do, but only practice can polish this much-needed skill.

You should break eye contact from time to time, maybe with a nod that shows agreement. Don't ever concentrate on the other person's facial flaws. We should avoid focusing on people's physical imperfections at all times, anyway—that's just common courtesy. Our job is to make people feel comfortable around us, not to make them want to avoid us as much as possible.

It is essential to focus on the person in front of you. Looking over someone's shoulder can be very distracting for both of you. This shows (even unintentionally) that you might be looking for someone or something more interesting than the person you're talking with. That will not establish a good reputation for you.

Your eyes shouldn't wander all over the other person's body or attire. If you would like to do so (say you really like the person's outfit and you want to check it out), you need to practice discretion. There is nothing worse than making the other person feel like an object instead of a future business partner.

When you enter a room, you shouldn't be laughing or giggling—this shows a light, flamboyant style that's unbecoming to a business professional. You need to be classy. There is nothing wrong with wanting to be perceived as down to earth, but being loud and lighthearted is not the ultimate winning approach.

When you introduce yourself, offer your hand to shake, make eye contact, and definitely smile when you greet the other person. This shows your friendly side and helps people feel at ease. It's also a way to be seen as an approachable individual, which gradually builds trust. It's a good idea to smile with your eyes as well. Some people don't like to smile openly, for various reasons, but smiling with your eyes can be a very inviting gesture and can definitely open up possibilities for communication.

There are many ways for you to practice these techniques: you can simply stand in front of a mirror at home and look at your face, trying to focus first on one eye, then the other. Practice smiling a little to see what kind of smile will be the most appropriate for networking events. Smile with your eyes and try, if you decide to have a wide smile, to be authentic and genuine. You even can practice not staring at the other person with your family members.

Believe it or not, people can sense how sincere you are from your facial expressions. There is no need to be nervous when meeting someone! It's fine to feel more excited than nervous—you just need to distinguish which one you're experiencing.

The Handshake

It's almost impossible to understate how important this is, in business relationships and in life. The handshake has been practiced as far back as the fifth century BC in ancient Greece. It signified peace and friendliness, showing that you didn't carry a weapon in your hand. In today's society, a good handshake sets the tone for business and communication in general. In American culture, the handshake is an extremely important ritual. There are many different kinds of handshakes, and they indicate different aspects of who you are, as a human and as a professional. Back in the day, a good handshake was actually your résumé—it was good enough to get you a job or to seal a contract.

To me, a good handshake represents:

1. Trust
2. Honesty
3. Integrity
4. Balance
5. Equality
6. Sincerity
7. Being interested and involved in our meeting
8. Openness
9. Confidence
10. Good manners

Using the right hand for a handshake is considered proper etiquette. Of course, in some cultures the handshake might not be as important, and in others the handshake might not be appropriate between people of different genders. Always do your research about cultural differences before traveling abroad for business.

Your next task is to write down five essential points of what a good handshake represents for you. Also, list why it is important, or if it isn't, why not.

1.
2.
3.
4.
5.

Handshake styles (good and bad)

Now that we know what a proper handshake means, let's learn how to do it correctly. You will need to extend your right arm with the thumb up. The hands should meet web to web (the space between the thumb and index finger), and the grip needs to be strong but not overwhelming. Give it just a couple of pumps.

Next, let's talk about some of the handshakes you should avoid because they often convey a message that might not work in your favor.

Dr. Gregory Stebbins' book, *People Savvy*, identifies ten different handshake types which actually reveal your personality. If you learn to read those handshake signals, you'll know who to conduct business with and how to handle different situations based on the handshake of your future client or business partner. Here are just a few well-known examples:

1. Sweaty palms: sometimes we can be a bundle of nerves, which will likely show up in our handshake. When introduced to a nervous or shy person, we need to make sure to put him at ease, which already indicates that we will be "the leading" partner in this communication.
2. "Dead fish": one of the most common and least favored handshakes you will encounter in your business relationships. This handshake feels like the person doesn't have strength in their hands. Accord-

ing to Dr. Stebbins's research, individuals with this kind of handshake are not very people oriented, so you need to focus mainly on subjects instead of "people topics" with them. Some people in very specific professional fields favor this handshake: often, musicians and surgeons do not prefer a firm handshake or refrain from "bone-crushing" handshakes to protect their hands.

3. Hand-over-hand (The Politician): this is a very interesting handshake which, if it's translated correctly, can show a lot about the relationship between you and the other individual. This handshake has to be performed between close friends or people who know each other because it can give mixed signals. Why is that? This handshake can show closeness, that you are important to the individual who shakes

your hand, or that he is thankful and grateful to be around you. It could also indicate that the person is trying to patronize you, manipulate you, or nurture you.

4. Bone-crusher: this is a very unpleasant handshake for the person on the receiving end. This is beyond a firm handshake and can actually hurt your bones. The person who uses this kind of a handshake is trying to show you his over-the-top business orientation, attempting to compensate for some kind of incompetence, or just simply showing aggression and trying to show you who's boss. Of course, by showing intimidation and power, he can only go wrong.

What is your handshake style? How does it work for you?

Posture

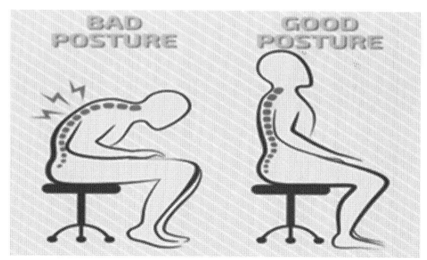

We all know the saying that we have only one chance to make a good first impression. How you present yourself is extremely important, which makes your posture a significant nonverbal communication skill.

There are two easily recognized postures: open and closed. Closed posture is never a good one, especially when you're meeting someone for the first time or if you want to make a good first impression. If your arms are crossed in front of your chest, this can indicate that you are bored, annoyed, or consider yourself better than the other person. At the same time, it can also indicate defensiveness.

An open posture is always preferable, as this indicates to the person in front of you that you are interested, connected, and present in the conversation—in general, that you are interested in meeting the person. Everyone likes to communicate with engaged people.

The best posture is standing straight and tall, with your arms next to your torso. Your head needs to be up, as well as your chin. Try not to overdo it, though, because you might be perceived as arrogant. Your arms should be comfortably back—if you have slouchy arms, this tends to shows that you're timid, not confident enough, and in general trying to minimize your importance. If you don't see yourself as important, it's likely that no one else will take you seriously.

Your posture should convey the message that you're approachable, warm, connected, confident, and natural. Looking "in control" can bring you a lot of opportunities.

Note: Some people may present themselves as not confident enough because they might want to make you feel superior in their company. However, this might be a tricky, subtle attempt to try to get a better deal by making you believe that they are vulnerable and weak, so you must learn to recognize many different business postures and styles. I believe that for some people intuition can help a great deal in this regard; of course, for many people this comes with experience.

Personal Space

As T. Hall, author of *The Hidden Dimension*, suggests, people often base their communication on personal space, which can have a profound effect on relationships.

Every culture has its own differences regarding personal space. In the United States, we are generally very respectful of personal space: this is our "personal bubble," and we feel violated if someone invades it. There are a few norms we should consider regarding personal space, and we tend to follow four major personal space charts:

1. Intimate distance—between six and eighteen inches. This distance often indicates a close relationship and high comfort zone.

2. Personal distance—between two to four feet or a little less. This is typical for family members and close friends.
3. Social distance—three to ten feet. This is preferable for acquaintances and the office environment.
4. Public distance—used for public speaking.

The space between intimate and personal distance is called *personal space*. Many people do consider this *their space*—one which no one should invade—and they might feel uncomfortable, angry, or frustrated if someone invades their "bubble." Unfortunately, many people are not familiar with the concept of personal space.

In the U.S., we have our own particular norms regarding personal space. What we consider to be appropriate in our culture might not be appropriate in other cultures. Personal space might vary based on familiarity and gender, as well as religious norms. In the U.S., we shake hands, keeping an arm's-length distance between people in business situations and at networking events. By contrast, in the Middle East, it is common for people of the same gender to exchange kisses, but men and women don't shake hands because Muslims refrain from touching the opposite sex.

Sometimes we need to forfeit a little bit of our own comfort and adjust to the other person's understanding of personal space in order to make the other person feel at ease. This indicates respect and understanding. One example was when President George W. Bush held hands and exchanged a friendly kiss with the late King Abdullah of Saudi Arabia. There was a lot of talk about it at the time, but since this is a standard Saudi custom, President Bush felt comfortable in the presence of the late Saudi king and reciprocated his gesture of kindness. Even if certain behaviors seem unusual, etiquette requires that you try your best to put the other person at ease. If you are sincere in being polite and well mannered, that's all that matters.

In 2009, First Lady Michelle Obama and Queen Elizabeth of England caused quite a buzz in the media all over the world when they shared a rare public moment of affection. When the First Lady hugged the queen, the monarch refrained from the usual strict protocol as well and returned the hug. This was a warm, friendly, open gesture between the two women. In fact, it was reported that the queen hugged Mrs. Obama first.

Another surprising moment happened in 2010 when Mrs. Obama shook hands with Indonesia's Information Minister, Tifatul Sembiring. After this was questioned by his countrymen, Sembiring said that he never touches women who are not relatives and that he had basically been forced into it: "I tried to prevent with my hands, but Mrs. Michelle held her hands too far toward me, we touched," he wrote on his Twitter account.

I could give many more examples of differently perceived personal-space moments, but in most instances, protocol is strictly followed. Of course, the rules can be changed (even unintentionally at times), especially when both parties are willing to accommodate each other and their behavior is not seen as intrusive or reckless. Media will talk, no matter what. That's their job.

Smile

Your smile is one of your most important nonverbal communication tools. Many people think that smiling might present them as weak, but actually, a person who smiles is perceived as more trustworthy (even if it's untrue), attractive, friendly, and open for communication. Your smiling face sends positive signals that attract people to you. Have you ever seen an angry, rude, bitter salesman who was successful at selling his products? Maybe online, but not likely in person. Your smile can actually be detected on the phone and even on social media. If you're a happy person, you won't be able to hide it. Of course, if you're not, it will be even harder for you to create the perception that you are.

A smile is your greatest means of introduction when you're at a networking event, but it's not a good idea to walk around giggling or laughing for no particular reason. When you meet a new person, especially in business situations, you need to stand up straight, offer a firm handshake, and smile at the person you're meeting. Your smile should be sincere and genuine. Of course, when we're dealing with negative emotions, it's really hard to smile, but to handle negativity with grace, it helps to at least try to smile. It might even make you feel better.

You can learn to smile. If you don't know how to smile yet, you need to make it a priority. You can actually start by practicing in front of a mirror and making it a habit. It takes about twenty-one days for something to become a habit, so if you practice smiling every single day, it will become an easy habit in less than a month.

Smile means "happiness" all over the world. Start using your smile as much as you can, and you'll definitely see a positive difference in your life.

We usually relate better to people who smile because they seem more open, friendly, and easy to be around. They look positive and energetic just because they smile! Your personality will determine how likable you are, and you can learn to be likable. Just smile more often!

Tone of Voice

Our tone of voice conveys 35 to 40 percent of our message. If there is a contradiction between the words we speak and the tone we use, people will believe the tone of voice before the content of what we say.

From an etiquette perspective, we always need to realize that speaking loudly, especially in public, is just plain rude. People around us don't need (or want) to know our business or hear our conversations. Speaking loudly intrudes on other people's space.

Many times, people with deeper voices are perceived as having greater authority, influence, perspective, and credibility. For women in business, it is very important to realize that a "baby doll" voice won't be accepted well. Of course, as females, we don't want to try to fake an unnatural, deep, manly voice—that would just seem odd—but if we speak slowly and confidently in a slightly lower register (without breathiness), this could have a positive effect on our business influence. Another important technique is to speak clearly—not too fast and not too slow. The point is always for the other person to be able to understand what we are trying to say.

Mimicking

This is another great technique to use when you're communicating with someone. They say that opposites attract, but this doesn't really apply in business relationships. We subconsciously tend to like people who resemble us (in this case, people who communicate like we do), so it's best to mirror the style of the person you're talking with. For example, if someone speaks slower than you do, it is a good idea to sync your tempo with theirs. If the person speaks clearly, you should speak clearly as well. This should all be done very discreetly and within limits. If the person speaks with a foreign accent or a different dialect, that doesn't mean you should try to copy it—you might be perceived as trying to make fun of or mock the other individual. Always use your best judgment and common sense.

Remembering Names

This is an essential part of making your first impression. We meet a lot of people every day, and it can be very difficult to remember all their names, but you can practice increasing your memory. When you meet someone, try to associate the person's name with something that's easy to remember, like a type of food or a TV personality. It also helps to say the person's name when you're introduced and several more times during your conversation. If you are listening to a conversation, you might be able to remember the person's name by repeating it in your head at least three times.

Even with memory-building exercises, we still forget people's names. How do you ask a person what his name is again and again? Try to remember the place you met before or associate your meeting with someone you both know. An understanding, polite person usually won't take it too personally and will remind you of their name.

Some people have difficult, complicated names. You can ask them to spell it out for you instead of just pretending you "got it" and start mispronouncing it or using it in the wrong way. Some people don't care, but most people do. That's why you should at least try to remember the person's name. Some foreign names might be more complicated than others, so sometimes the other person will give you a shortened version or tell you how they'd like to be addressed. I usually try to remember the full version of the person's name—it's always more authentic and shows genuine interest.

Now we know the most important basic details involved in a proper, poised introduction. Let's recap what we've learned:

1. When you meet someone, stand up and shake the other person's hand firmly.
2. Make and maintain appropriate eye contact.
3. Smile!
4. Maintain an appropriate amount of personal space.
5. Use a pleasant tone of voice.
6. Try to remember the person's name by using techniques to refresh your memory.

VERBAL COMMUNICATION

Listening skills

One of the most important (possibly *the* most important) skills in communication is listening well. To be a great communicator (which is crucial for the success of every single business), we need to learn to listen better. Fortunately, there are a few techniques we can learn to help us become great listeners.

Forget about yourself for a few minutes. The person in front of you should have your complete attention. You need to be present. In my experience, we miss opportunities because we lose the connection, and that happens when we aren't focused and fully attentive to the conversation we're having. People can always tell if we're genuinely interested in them. Even if we're not, we need to be polite and show respect.

We think at the rate of about six hundred words per minute, but most people only speak about 160 words per minute. If you're caught up in listening to your own thoughts, you won't be able to hear the other person's part of the conversation. It's easy to do, but don't think about your answers while the other person is talking—that's a guaranteed way to lose the connection very easily. Your answers probably wouldn't be relevant anyway because you missed half of what the other person was trying to say. Don't get me wrong; you need to make an equal contribution to the conversation, but you won't be able to do that if you aren't *really* listening to what's being said.

Remember, people like to be acknowledged. In their

eyes, they have important information to offer you. When you give them the opportunity to present their viewpoint, you're likely to learn something *and* position yourself well to build a strong business relationship with them. Business is based on relationships, and making someone feel comfortable around you simply by listening creates a win-win situation.

For most of my adult life, I have lived in foreign countries and had some insecurity about pronouncing certain words correctly or understanding the correct lingo for a particular situation or culture. This made me a very good listener. So sometimes what seems like a problem can turn out to work for you in mysterious ways. Use them to your advantage.

Make sure to use your body language to show people that you're actively listening. Lean towards the person or even change seats to get closer. Never turn your back; that's extremely rude and inconsiderate. Ignore your cell phone if it rings. You can raise your eyebrows, but make sure it's not in a sarcastic way. Smile when it's appropriate. If the person talks about something really sad or a subject he's bothered about, just go with the conversation. That's why it is important to pay attention.

Nod from time to time, say a few words like "hmm" or "I see" to signal that you're paying attention, and show that you agree or disagree in a very mellow manner. Try to laugh at the person's jokes, even if they aren't that funny, but be very careful about being sincere. Sometimes a chuckle or a grin will do just fine. We all have different levels of humor based on our culture, upbringing, and perceptions.

Small Talk

When you meet someone, you want to send a nice, warm vibe. One way to do this is by engaging in "small talk." Even though it's called "small," the results can be pretty significant. Why? Because based on small talk, you can get an idea about people's personalities, habits, family situation, hobbies, etc. Sometimes knowing a little bit more about a person helps you find a way to connect.

It's always good to be up to date on sports, movies, international news, interesting facts, or local exhibitions. You can talk about your love of pets to find out if the person is a fellow animal lover. If you're both interested in sports but the other person supports a team you don't like, you can certainly have your opinion, but don't be rude about it. You're trying to look for positive things to talk about with other people, not subjects to argue about. You can talk about favorite foods, movies you've seen recently, or a great book.

Many people talk about the weather, which is a classic way to start small talk. Even though it's a good conversation starter, this can quickly become boring because we can all see the weather through the window. Try to talk about something interesting, but remember that although some topics might be really interesting to you, they may not be as fascinating for the person you're talking to. If the other person asks you a question, try to answer with full sentences while being friendly and inviting. You can always end the conversation with a question as well.

Write down five of your favorite topics that you might choose the next time you need to employ small talk in conversation. Read about them and increase your knowledge so you'll bring something unique to the table. Some topics might not be great subjects for this type of casual communication, so consider the situation and the person you'll be talking to.

Here are some great topics for small talk:

Books—find out if the person is interested in reading and books in general. I love reading, and this is very appealing to me. When I find someone with the same interests, I will be even more likely to keep in touch with them. If the person doesn't really like to read, I'm sure there must be something else we can talk about.

A particular neighborhood—where we live, would love to live, or a place that has an interesting reputation. For example, I've learned through small talk which areas are the best to take my kids trick or treating.

Travel adventures—if you travel a lot and the other person doesn't, you can always suggest someplace that was intriguing, surprising, pleasant, or even not so wonderful. I always like to share my experiences in South Africa, Northern Africa, and Europe. When I talk about South Africa, I can share interesting information about different foods I tested there or the trips I took through Kruger National Park. People who love nature and travel relate very well to those topics. Be sure to share your adventures in a modest way. It's never okay to brag, sharing how much the hotel cost or how amazing it was to travel in business class while the losers were all back in economy class. This won't make you popular, and it certainly won't establish your reputation in a good way.

Favorite foods—this is a topic that can help you find out very interesting information about the person in front

of you. Some people don't eat pork, which might be an indication that they practice a particular religion. That might give you a hint about which topics you can talk about and which you should avoid. If you're like me, you have vegetarian friends who love animals; this could direct you to the topic of compassion among pet lovers. When you talk about things people love and are passionate about, more people will like you, and when more people like you, you have more potential customers. It's even better if you are genuinely interested in many different topics. I love to listen and learn about topics I don't know much about. Many times we put up filters, believing that we're really not interested in a certain area, but even if you aren't familiar with the topic, give it a try—it could turn out to be a very interesting conversation for everyone involved.

Sports—people say that when you find out what kind of sports a person is interested in, you can find out many traits regarding their personality. I love tennis and swimming, along with a lot of other sports. I'm always surrounded by people, and as a single mom with two kids, I need a little space from time to time, so that's why I love swimming. I do like to be alone with my thoughts at times, and swimming offers me a little escape from the daily routine of life. To many people, my love of swimming might indicate that I am a loner or someone who isn't a team player, but my experience shows that it's usually dangerous to generalize, because I like basketball, too.

List five interesting topics you might want to share with someone else. You can practice them at home with your friends or family members. You might think that you have nothing interesting to share with the world, but we all do. You just need to find it inside of you. You need to write it down and visualize it. I write down everything I do or am planning to do—I need to be able to "see" it. Always remember, common sense is not always common practice, and even if someone doesn't respond to your communication techniques the way you would like them to, that doesn't necessarily mean that your topic is boring or you're a bad conversationalist. Many times the problem lies with them. Even if it's the other way around, don't get discouraged; you'll get to the level you need to be.

1.

2.

3.

4.

5.

CHAPTER SEVEN

Business Attire

If you're looking for a job, already have a job, or are trying to get promoted, you will always need to observe a particular dress code. It doesn't matter how eloquent your vocabulary is, how skilled you are in the field, or how many degrees you have, you need to be appropriately dressed, professional, and polished. Once you learn a few basic but crucial lessons about attire, you'll be able to dress better than ever. You can always create your own combinations and impress the world with your style.

If you're looking for a job, you need to find out what kind of company you are applying to. You can always ask the HR manager or the receptionist what the dress code is for the company. You can research the company online to determine what is appropriate for that industry.

Pay attention to the size of the company. If it's a big company, you may be able to be a little more flexible. You can look successful, which will show the interviewers that you aren't desperate and that you'd fit right in at their company. If the job interview is with a smaller company, you may wish to dress more modestly; don't be flashy. You don't want to look desperate, but you also don't want to look like someone who's just looking for a job out of boredom.

COLOR

Color has major psychological effects on us, and the business world is no exception. Different colors influence people in a very different ways. Your choice of color can strongly represent the personality you are trying to portray. How you want to be perceived is very much up to you. You are conveying certain subliminal message through the colors you chose.

Some specific colors match a particular perception that most people share: red means stop, green means go. Red represents being alert, getting attention, and acting with an immediate effect. In business, when we hear the phrase, "you have the green light," we know that means to go ahead and continue on with what we are doing to get the project done. It may be very difficult to change the meaning of colors in our imagination because we've learned to associate the color with certain common activities they represent.

Many times colors can have a gender connotation as well. In today's vibrant, constantly changing society, the association between gender and color seems more minimized than in days past. We are all used to the idea that pink represents female and blue represents male, but nowadays it's quite fashionable for men to wear pink, and women wear blue all the time.

In business, we need to consider the company's culture. If we will be conducting a job interview or business meeting in a conservative environment, then the colors listed below are our best bets. The fact that many businesspeople wear these colors doesn't mean that you absolutely have to wear them as well. You may feel more comfortable in different colors, but just keep in mind that, in the business world, conservative colors are preferred. Choose the one that suits your personality and use your styling sense in the best possible way.

The most popular colors for both genders are blue, gray, and black.

Blue

Blue is the most popular and widely used color in business. You're probably not surprised that blue is predominant in the logos of Facebook, Twitter, LinkedIn, the NFL, and many more businesses whose revenues range in the billions of dollars. Blue represents innovation, efficiency, clear mind, structured thinking, trust, and influence. The color by itself won't make you successful, but it conveys a particular message to those who see it, and you can express your knowledge successfully through your image.

Blue is one of the most often recommended colors for job interviews. It conveys trustworthiness, loyalty, calm, and the image that you are in control of the situation. Many diplomats, bankers, world dignitaries, and members of royalty wear the color blue.

This color can also help in concentration. Some studies advise that too much of some particular shades of blue could promote feelings of sadness or even depression, so, just like every other color, blue should be used in moderation.

Gray

Gray is a beautiful color—very stylish, conservative, sophisticated, and classic. The color gray conveys neutrality as a subliminal message. However, in some situations, like if you're applying for an upper-level position in management, it might send the message that you're neutral and might not be ready to take on enough responsibility.

Many times, though, being "neutral" without trying hard to attract attention might benefit you. You might become more recognizable than other people in our "me" society, where everybody craves attention. Gray is a "confident" color as well, and it represents knowledge, intelligence, and wisdom.

Black

This is a very strong, formal, widely used color. Many people like to wear black for business events. This color represents authority and power. At the same time, if it's used too much, it could be overpowering. I always suggest (especially for ladies) that if you join an evening business meeting or networking event after 5:00 p.m., refrain from wearing black for the simple reason that 90 percent of the women there will also be wearing black. If you want to stand out, choose something else.

Black can also have a demanding and controlling connotation. It is definitely not a cheerful color. At the same time, black can be an extremely useful color because it is a good match with pretty much any other color.

STYLE

“ *Simplicity is the ultimate sophistication.* **”**

—Leonardo da Vinci

You can look classy, refined, and successful by "editing" your look. In other words, follow the motto "less is more." Fashion always changes, but in business scenarios, there are a few rules every professional should follow. Many times the wrong choice definitely sends the wrong message. It's not that complicated to dress well. It's a question of a good taste, and taste can be developed. There are a few rules or points we might want to follow by learning how to look our best in different occasions.

Classics vs Trends

One of the most important things to do when you dress to impress is to develop your own style by choosing between classics and trends. It's easy to get carried away by modern elements and pop culture. We need to remember that just because something is considered fashionable doesn't mean it will look good on us (or on anyone else, for that matter).

What does "classic" actually mean? Classic is "the fashion" which never goes out of style. The pieces which represent "the classic" trend are those that look good on almost everyone. They might have had little or no changes over time, but you can never go wrong by wearing them; their success has been tested and proven over the years.

What's your perfect fit?

When you're choosing your outfit, don't be a slave to the size chart. You may think you're a size 6 or 12, but sizes aren't consistent at every store or with every garment you purchase. How can you determine the best size for you? When you purchase any new piece of clothing, try on the size you normally buy, then try on one size smaller and one size larger. By trying all three, you'll see which one looks best on you. Try to see yourself from all sides. You want to look great from every angle. And don't forget your undergarments! They're equally important as the outer clothes you wear because they can make or break the look. Be very mindful of that.

When I was younger, I liked a particular piece of clothing that was two sizes too small for me, but I bought it anyway in the hope that by the end of the year I would be able to fit into it. Are you guilty of doing that, too, or it is just me? I think this was because I wasn't happy with my size at the time (and many people are not). I suggest that you don't make the same mistake. Clothes go out of style, and you're just wasting your money if they don't fit. I don't buy "future" clothes anymore because it's a waste of money and energy. No one is perfect, so we must try to work around our imperfections.

When I was a child, my grandfather used to say, "I am not rich enough to buy cheap things," and this saying has stayed with me ever since. Another important thing to remember is "We get what we pay for." In most cases, these statements are true. In other words, if you would like something to last longer, you should invest in better quality materials to begin with. You can build your ideal wardrobe little by little. You don't have to wait forever to create the proper wardrobe, but you can start somewhere.

The importance of the correct fabric

The fabrics you use to create your best look are essential! The way you combine the essential clothing characteristics can give you a classy, beautiful outfit or it can make you look like a clown. Remember; less is always more in this department.

During the colder winter months, try to wear clothes made of wool, heavier cotton, and other textures that keep you warm while still being stylish for the season. Colors are also important. I believe we can all wear white after Labor Day if it is not our summer white cotton dress or our white beach shorts (for people who wear shorts). The same goes for the gentlemen. Your summer linen white pants will be a very bad choice, but your off-white cashmere sweater could be a perfect choice. We wear linen during the summer because it is a very light material that's perfect for hot months.

We also need to be careful in combining colors and patterns. Color combinations can bring out the best in us or create an unforgettable caricature. Some colors can make us look slimmer, taller, and, combined with the right pattern, can achieve the best look for us. Black and vertical stripes can definitely be slimming, but horizontal stripes, especially in combination with light colors, can have the complete opposite effect.

Learn what your best feature is and accentuate it. You can also hide something that you don't like about your appearance. For example, if you'd like to look taller, a black dress with long sleeves will do the trick. If you think you look too tall and you'd like to look a little shorter, wear an outfit with two different colors—for example, a dark blue skirt and a white blouse. This will create the illusion that you're shorter.

One of the best pieces of advice about how to choose colors that work for you comes from one of the most prominent etiquette experts, Elena Neitlich:

Those colors that painters study, while trying to represent individual skin tones, occur as a result of pigments in our skin, hemoglobin, melanin, and carotene. We are each born with a particular combination of these pigments.

You need to figure out which color makes you look vibrant, alive, and visible when close to your face. From there, you'll be able to create your own palette of samples.

ACCESSORIES

Jewelry

The secret is always in the details. If you're wearing a conservative outfit in pastel or dark colors, some classy accessories could be a great accent. The jewelry needs to be tasteful and limited in number. Don't put rings on every finger. A stylish watch will always look extremely elegant and represents success. Stud earrings are best for women; in general, earrings should be very discreet for business situations. Hoops and long or feather-like earrings might be very appropriate in some industries (like retail or fashion), but never for business occasions. Don't wear too many bracelets because they could create unnecessary, distracting noise.

Men should refrain from wearing earrings at all times.

Other accessories

A nice belt, scarf, or briefcase will complete your outfit. Don't use too much perfume (or aftershave, for men), since some people might be allergic to them. Always apply the rule "less is more."

Shoes

Try to match your shoes with your purse (for women) or your belt (for men). Women, if you would like a pop of color, you can choose bright-colored shoes that complement your blouse.

For the modern businessman, *always* wear socks with your shoes. A good rule of thumb is if you're wearing a mid- to dark-colored suit such as navy, charcoal gray, or black, your socks should match your trouser color—think of your socks as an extension of your pants so that when they show, your image remains unified in appearance. If you're wearing a lighter colored suit, wear socks that match your shoe color.

Flip-flops are *never* okay in business situations. Even if you do business in Southern California, where I live, this is something to avoid at all times. Flip flops belong at the beach or at the pool.

Hairstyle

Your hairstyle is essential for creating that perfect look. Some styles are definitely not appropriate for the contemporary corporate environment, but they may be suitable for a more casual, modern type of atmosphere. Always research the company's culture first.

Take Care of Your Clothes

Your clothes should always be clean and well pressed. Every garment has care instructions included on the tag. If you aren't sure what to do, follow the instructions. Looking clean and sharp for a job interview or a business meeting is always more important than the price tag on your clothes. Pay attention to the little details.

Your hands

I'm not suggesting that men should get a manicure every week, but if you just changed the oil in your car, you'll definitely need to take care of your hands. You have to be clean at all times. Remember that you'll be shaking hands a lot, and if you present a product to a client on your laptop, the client will definitely look at your hands, so have nicely maintained nails.

For the ladies, I know that nail-industry trends are booming everywhere, but we need to understand what's appropriate for a business environment. Nails with diamonds, pearls, and bright colors, as well as very long nails, are definitely not the styles of choice. Simply put, they look unprofessional and tacky. You don't want to ever hear the question: "How do you work with such a long nails?"

DRESS CODES

When you receive an invitation to a party, business meeting, or any similar kind of event, the dress code will usually be written on the event invitation or sent in the email. Many people are profoundly confused by dress codes, so much so that they'll even skip the event because they don't have the necessary confidence or the correct clothing. Remember that conducting business, making a sale, or leading a successful meeting is always done when people connect, so the more people you meet, the better.

Most Common Dress Codes

Here are the four dress codes that are most often used in business situations and office environments.

1. *Casual*—this style reflects a relaxed environment. When people indicate on an invitation, in an email, or verbally that you should dress casually, this means that you can wear whatever you like, as long is appropriate, clean, and uncontroversial. Use your common sense. Of course, don't wear extremely revealing clothes or just a bathing suit.

2. *Business Casual*—this particular style is a step up in the "style register." Men can wear cotton twill pants (Dockers™ type), which must always well

pressed, and a nice button-down shirt, which can be open at the collar. Use colors that match and try to avoid bright combinations. Don't wear a tie. Shoes, as always, should be polished. Don't ever wear flip-flops, sandals, or sneakers.

Women can wear a two-piece ensemble (in the same color, with nice statement buttons). If the buttons are too bold, wear less jewelry. You want to project class and success, and in business fashion, less is always more. Instead of drawing attention with our appearance, we want to our conversation to be the focus, and too many details can be distracting. Wear colors that suit your complexion and bring out the best of your natural beauty.

You can always wear a nice pencil skirt. Pants are a comfortable choice as well. I recommend black because it goes with absolutely everything and makes for a classy look. You can complement your skirt or slacks with a nice fashionable blouse. If the blouse has ruffles, don't wear jewelry—maybe only stud earrings.

Shoes should have a closed toe and have a relaxed look—high heels and platforms will make you feel *and* look uncomfortable.

3. ***Business Formal/Semiformal/Informal***—for this style, men should wear classic suit, (make sure to take your suit to a dry cleaner often; you might have the most expensive-looking suit, but if doesn't smell fresh and look like it's well taken care of, that makes a bad statement about you). Always wear conservative col-

ors, and you'll never go wrong. Wear a pressed, button-down shirt and a tie. The tie should be tasteful. It can be chic, but avoid ties with bold elements, bright colors, flowers, or goofy images. Your tie can make a big impression by revealing a bit about your taste. Remember that everything makes a statement about you, positive or negative.

Of course, you should always wear a well-fitted jacket to complete your business formal look. Make sure your pieces match; we've all seen men whose jackets might be darker than their pants (or the other way around) because they didn't consistently wear them together. If some clothes are "too tired," then they need to "retire." It's a good idea to invest in a few pieces of high-quality clothing. Pay attention to your shoes—they need to always be polished and well maintained. Often your shoes reveal more about your success than your outfit does.

For female professionals, I suggest that if you're going for a more formal occasion in the evening, wear something besides black. This will make you stand out from the crowd. You can wear a nice suit, but be sure to choose the right fabric for the season. You might choose a beautiful dress which brings out the best of your features, and you can definitely wear higher-heeled shoes. In fact, it's advisable to wear elegant, classy shoes suitable for the occasion. Definitely keep in mind that you should not reveal too much skin. Don't wear very short hemlines, and make sure everything fits well. By all means, try on your outfit well in advance to make sure the clothes aren't too tight or too loose.

You can accentuate your makeup a bit more, but that doesn't mean you should overdo it. Pantyhose are always preferable if you're wearing a skirt and the weather conditions are suitable. Nude color is always the most elegant, but in the evening, you can wear black if it matches your outfit. Do not wear a white skirt with black stockings; it's not an aesthetically pleasing combination. Stay away from bright-colored or "sexy" stockings, too—it's still a business formal occasion.

4. *Festive attire*—this is considered appropriate for office parties or other times when we're celebrating with coworkers, business professionals, and business partners. This is when we decide to be more relaxed, have some fun, and celebrate occasions at the office. It's always best when we receive the invi-

tation early and have time to prepare for it.

For example, if the invitation calls for football attire, you can wear a football jersey and decorate the place with footballs. Try to celebrate team spirit. If some people wear gear from a football team you don't like, this is not the place for you to make disparaging remarks; in fact, it's the perfect time to make a special effort to be friendly and nice. Enjoy relaxing with your coworkers, and take the time to get to know them better.

Here's another example: if the celebration is for Cinco de Mayo, dress appropriately for the occasion. Wear prints that are associated with the celebration. Accentuate the Mexican-inspired designs and enjoy.

In most situations with festive attire, use your common sense and be careful not to go beyond the limits of good taste. Avoid things like super-heavy mascara and looking like a caricature—you don't want to be remembered as the person who left his limitations and common sense at home.

No matter what kind of occasion you're invited to, always, *always* compliment the host and offer your sincere thanks.

CHAPTER EIGHT

Cyber Civility and Your Presence

We live in a fast-paced, largely transparent and electronically influenced world. We do most of our business communication online, and almost all of us have some kind of social media presence, so we have to be careful about how we conduct ourselves when we communicate through cyberspace. It's easy if you just stick to the basic rules of etiquette: be respectful, kind, and considerate. Cyber civility is a regular form of civility, just used in a different way. The fact that we are behind a computer doesn't gives us the right to bully people or to be rude. We also shouldn't tolerate that kind of behavior in others.

Emails

This is one of the most common, widely used, and efficient methods of communication in business situations. If you're at the office, you're more likely to send an email response than to answer your business phone. There are established appropriate international business codes for email communication. Emails are a type of documentation and are electronically written evidence.

What do we need to know about utilizing emails?

When you send an email, always address the recipient politely. You can use the words "Dear so and so" up front. This is a very common approach in Europe. Always address the person by her last name, especially if you don't know her (i.e., "Dear Ms. Thompson"). The person will let you know how to address her in the next email. If the email is signed with the first and last name, then you should continue to address the person by her last name. If it's signed with only the first name, then you have the green light to address the individual by their first name. Make sure the name is spelled correctly. There is nothing more negligent than contacting a business person and making a silly mistake from the first moment. Your image is on the line.

When you receive an email, the polite thing to do is to respond within forty-eight hours. If you postpone your response longer than that, you will need to indicate why it took you so long to respond. At times, we do have valid reasons, but to be safe, try to respond within that time frame.

Your tone shouldn't be demanding, obnoxious, or rude. Always remember that people read between the lines. To end your email, say "Thank you," "You're welcome," and, especially if you're in the fast lane of customer service, "Is there anything else I can help you with?" We do business with people based not only on the products they sell, but also on the level of their customer service and the way they make us feel. You should be more reserved and polite in the business environment. This is always the most beneficial way to present yourself and your agenda.

People can tell if you're being rude or you're not particularly happy with what you do. Do not use all capital letters; in the cyber world, this is considered shouting. Use normal sentence structure with proper capitalization, grammar, and spelling. Don't use acronyms (e.g., LOL, etc.), since the person may not understand them unless it is well known, like NATO or the UN.

When you write an email, refrain from using abbreviations. For example, TGIF means "Thank God it's Friday" for people who are aware of it, but for the rest of us (yes, I was one of those), they're just strange letters. You can say "Happy Friday," of course. Using abbreviations is not professional, and the impression you project might not be the one you intend to.

I know many people are excited because most programs have a spell checker, but it won't be enough if you don't have good grammar and punctuation skills to begin with. Make sure to proofread your documents, materials, and letters before you send the email. If you aren't sure about these things, hire a proofreader to do this task for you. Often we're in such a rush to complete ten emails in three minutes that we don't take the time to check them twice. We want to make sure we sent the correct message. We all need to slow down, take our time, and check our emails before we send them. This should be a general rule when emailing anyone.

If you have time, you should evaluate your style of writing emails, or have a trusted friend or colleague help with it. In today's fast-paced business environment, we are busier than ever, which means if I receive a very long email, I might not be able to read it all, and then I could miss most of the important information I need to know. Can you blame me? If I get hundreds of emails every day, I will most likely just read the subject line and do a brief scan of the content. Long emails might simply be skipped over or left for a time of the day when I am not so busy, which means almost never.

The important thing here is to put the exact reason for the email in the subject line and continue it in the body of the email. You can use bullet points to mark the important elements you would like to highlight. This always works for me, and it will work for you as well. At the end of your email, put your contact information: name, phone number, website (if you are a business owner) and your social media handles. Make sure you are sending your professional media handles, not your personal ones. This can be put in your signature line, which shows up on every email you send out.

One very delicate and potentially dangerous thing to watch out for is forwarding something to a group without using the BCC field for the email addresses. Use group emails only if every recipient is included in it and should know who else received the email. Check who's been included previously in the email, because mistakes can happen, and it's easy to make an unnecessary remark that we mean for only one recipient, but it goes to everyone. It's best to "strip out" all email addresses that may be in the body of the email you are forwarding. The "reply all" option is very useful and can save tons of time, but we still need to be very much aware of who we are replying to. Slow down, read it through several times, and then send the reply, forward, CC, or BCC to the appropriate persons. When forwarding any kind of information, be sure to be polite and professional.

It's very important not to engage in controversial conversations via email, especially if you are not 100 percent sure what the discussion is all about. Take some time to reflect. Clarify the subject and the conversation, and then you can get engaged if you really have to.

Some employees aren't capable of handling their own struggles and feel the need to CC their bosses when they want to put their coworkers on the spot. I'm sure we've all worked with these kinds of people. If you're one of them, please stop. It's unethical and can definitely backfire at some point. Besides, people watch you, and they build their impression of you based on your ethical (or unethical) behavior.

Conference calls

Be informed about when and where the conference call will take place so you'll be punctual and prepared. Nobody likes people interrupting conference calls because they're late. This can confirm a good impression as well, because being on time shows commitment. Punctuality is one of the most essential etiquette skills.

Always introduce yourself. Speak clearly and loud enough for everyone to hear you. Depending on the capacity of the meeting, you should mention the company and the department you represent.

Don't interrupt with questions; there will be time during or after the conference call when you can present your questions or concerns. The person who facilitates the call will let everybody know the appropriate time for questions and answers. In the meantime, take notes and be prepared when the time does come for your burning questions.

If you're by yourself in a room or office, make sure (especially if you're not on mute) not to make funny noises, eat, or listen to music. Don't make disrespectful or rude remarks. You always need to be present and show respect to everybody involved in the conference call.

When you lead a conference call, you should establish a length for the call. If the initial decision is two hours, you should do your best to fit into the two-hour time frame. If there is increasingly escalating discussion regarding a hot topic, you should ask if the participants would like to stay longer, but don't make it mandatory.

Facebook

According to Statista.com, in the first quarter of 2016, Facebook had 1.65 billion monthly active users, and this number is growing rapidly. Facebook is an incredible platform which can be extremely helpful if used correctly and very detrimental if used in the wrong way. If you are a business professional, always remember to use your business page most of the time for business conversations. Your personal page is for your personal life. We all know that our "personal" page is very public on FB, so we need to be mindful of the content we do share. We can't bully or be malicious, rude, or unethical at any time. Some people might push your buttons based on their personal understanding and beliefs, but this doesn't mean you need to get involved into a heated dispute.

If you'd like FB to work for you in an appropriate manner, there are a few norms you should be aware of. Whenever you like a post, you can like it and *then* share it. Don't share information without acknowledging the person who posted it first. You can make a brief comment as well.

When somebody likes your posts, it's good manners to reciprocate the attention, at least from time to time. We're living in a "me" society, and people can sometimes take themselves too seriously.

It's okay to send a request asking people to like your page, but if you do send the request, please don't send another request immediately just to advertise your events or products. This is the worst possible way to build a clientele. You need to exchange some information first and try to build understanding and brief relationships at the very least. I usually "unfollow" or "unfriend" people who send sales requests immediately after I accept their page request.

Another extremely annoying behavior is when you add people to groups you belong to. You can't just add people to groups without their personal consent. This is rude, unprofessional, and never builds revenue, if you ask me.

If you manage to find personal information about someone you're interested in pursuing as a client, do *not* call their personal cell phone directly. This is extremely intrusive behavior and could be perceived as creepy, dangerous, and offensive. If the phone number is on the website, then go ahead and call. If not, *don't.*

If you'd like to tag someone in your post, do so if the content includes the person you're tagging, the person you're tagging is interested in the content, or the person is a close friend of yours. Some people get really overwhelmed by too many tags.

You can engage in small conversations with people who aren't on your close friends list; just be polite. I'm always surprised when people are shocked when someone who isn't in their close contacts leaves a brief comment. Well, if you would like only seven of your thousand contacts to acknowledge, you probably shouldn't be on social media.

LinkedIn

Ahh, those endorsements! Sometimes we need to be really careful about offering them, because if we don't know the person well, it might look unprofessional. For example, if you see "public speaking" as an endorsement option, just make sure the person is really great at public speaking. I have friends who absolutely hate public speaking and never choose to do it, but they still get endorsed for it. Try to be sincere, and don't do this just because you're looking for endorsements in return.

LinkedIn is a professional social media site, but there are still people who get confused about the purpose. It's not a dating platform, so try to be professional, polite, and uncontroversial.

Your profile picture is very important, so use a classy, professional photo. Usually a head shot is a good choice.

When someone sends you a note congratulating you for a particular accomplishment, respond and thank the person for their attention.

I definitely disconnect with people who contact me via my business email with requests to watch their promotional videos or buy their products from the first moment I accept their friend request. It is very rude and unprofessional.

I focused on Facebook and LinkedIn above, but the rules are pretty much the same for all communication through social media.

CHAPTER NINE

Networking

According to the dictionary, networking is "a supportive system of sharing information and services among individuals and groups having common interests." Networking is paramount for success in the twenty-first century. If you know how to collaborate with people, then your opportunities are endless. We have all probably read, or at least heard of, Dale Carnegie's *How to Win Friends and Influence People*, which was first published in 1936. Many critics have criticized the approach as too simplistic, emphasizing good manners, etiquettes and sometimes suggesting manipulative techniques just to get ahead professionally. We don't want to manipulate anybody, but we definitely *can* become influencers. Good manners, politeness, and etiquette techniques work in most situations. Carnegie's book sold more than fifteen million copies worldwide, so there must be some value in the ideas.

I consider etiquette the "sharpest" soft skill of the twenty-first century. In today's constantly changing economy, good manners and etiquette rituals are not enough, because after we learn everything "by the book"—how to communicate with people and bring them into our corner—we still have to carry it through to the end, and we need to be able to present great content and prove ourselves in many ways, both in business and personal life.

Traditional Networking

Traditional forms of networking include the typical events, spaces, conferences, seminars, luncheons, dinners, etc. The most essential thing to remember while using traditional ways of networking is to project *confidence but not arrogance*. There's a very thin line between the two.

Do not skip the reception table. If the event requires name tags, this is where you will receive yours.

Name tags should be worn on the right side. When you shake another person's hand, the eye slides through the hand and down the arm directly to the name tag, reminding you of the person's name.

Always hold your glass in your left hand, since it's normal to shake with the right hand. That way you won't need to switch hands when you introduce yourself.

Do your homework. What's the reason you're attending the event? Find out who else will be attending. You don't need to introduce yourself to everyone, but you do need to meet the person you're going there to meet.

Approach groups while you're there. Don't miss an important event just because no one else you know will be attending. During the event, approach groups larger than two people (two people might be having a personal conversation). Stick around the group, listen to the conversation, and try to participate when it will be meaningful. At a suitable moment, you can introduce yourself.

Be proactive. Don't wait for the people around you—create opportunities for them to meet you. If you were invited, you have something to offer. Don't feel intimidated in any way. You're already on the right path.

Social Media

This form of networking can include everything from Facebook to Instagram, Twitter, LinkedIn, Pinterest, blogging, and so on. Social media gives us the opportunity to "meet" as many people as we wish on a daily basis and spread our message or our name as far as we can, sometimes further than we can even imagine.

Believe me, as a person who networks on a daily basis, I advise you to do as much networking as you can. Of course, both networking styles have their pluses and minuses. The traditional ways are more personal and deep; you can associate more actively with people, sense their personality, and create a strong connection. This is the positive part of traditional networking. Unfortunately, it doesn't allow us to meet 150 new people every day or spread our messages on all seven continents in one day. It's limited in this regard.

I've been using both of the techniques for a long time, and if you manage to incorporate your networking knowledge diligently and intelligently, I am convinced that you'll enjoy success beyond measure. In the twenty-first century, many people often hear the suggestion to "create your own economy." But how can this happen? You need to be an immaculate communicator and an expert influencer. You need to learn, practice, and implement the skills you need to prepare for the situations you'll face, and it will get easier moment by moment.

I've had the opportunity to travel the world and be invited to many social and business networking events. In the beginning, I felt very shy, intimidated, and insecure. The point is to start somewhere and open up. We sometimes need to push ourselves further and further, realizing that anything we do happens only through communication, whether it's looking for a job, climbing higher on the professional ladder, being an entrepreneur, making sales, or just meeting people because we want to be in a certain social circle.

Identify Your Networking Style

In my experience as a business professional and entrepreneur, I've found that people use at least one of the three networking styles listed below. Most people actually mix certain elements from different styles, and as soon as you recognize what works best for you and your industry, you should develop your own "ideal" working style. Your self-awareness is one of your most valuable skills. If you can learn as much as possible about your networking style (based on your personality), you'll be much more able to position yourself where you'd like to be.

A valuable first step is to recognize your own networking style. After you've figured this out, you'll be able to build relationships based on that style. There is no perfect style; you just need to remember that it's much better to be authentic and turn your style into the first step to winning new friends, business partners, and customers. Everything you do is a networking opportunity: going to a party, baby shower, seminar, networking group, even going to the office. The way you present yourself can make or break your reputation.

1. Competitive Networking Style—"action-oriented and direct communicators, motivated by fast and measurable results" (according to Don Gabor, author, communications trainer, and small talk expert). It's not difficult to recognize people with this particular networking style. I'm sure many of us have met people with this demanding way of communicating. They are usually very confident and easygoing, they don't take "no" for an answer, and they demand attention. Many of them talk more than they listen, and they expect everyone to be extremely amused and mesmerized by their achievements.

   Is this your style? If so, you might want to consider changing it. Some people are more attracted by lower-key presentations, and we all know that one very important, powerful technique in networking and communicating is listening. People who possess this aggressive style expect *you* to listen to (and agree with) *them*. It's easy to miss an opportunity to create a genuine connection and find people who really like you for who you are. In fact, this type of personality might be perceived as aggressive, and business professionals might choose to stay away from you.

2. Extroverted Networking Style—"people oriented and friendly communicators." People who network using this style are easygoing, put everyone around them at ease, and feel comfortable in almost every social and business situation. They have a high level of confidence, but knowing their networking power,

they can usually win you over by making small talk about subjects that *you* like and showing genuine interest in your business, personality, products, and just about everything you present to them. They can create opportunities for everyone, and they have a win-win attitude. Usually they are very positive, goal-oriented people, and they can mingle with individuals from different social circles and walks of life. Being so friendly and intrigued by everyone you meet might drain your energy or dilute your focus, and you might waste a lot of valuable time meeting people and connecting just to communicate without any valuable results. The energy needed for this networking style has to be directed and funneled properly to generate results.

3. Introverted Networking Style—these people are usually shy and not willing to dive into a conversation first, but they can open up when they feel they can trust you. Many introverted individuals have a high level of knowledge in a certain field, and many times they are completely absorbed by their work. If you manage to build trust with them, they'll often open up, and they can be extremely loyal team players. They are generally very reliable and willing to work hard. They find it difficult to attend networking events, especially if they don't know anyone there, which can be a reason for them to miss great business opportunities. They love their work and rarely go for the award or recognition. Because of the nature of their character, you will have to be the

initiator when it comes to connecting with them. They might have a great intellect, but if they do not utilize the power of networking, their product might go unnoticed.

Your Business Card and Your Image

Business cards are an internationally recognized way to exchange information and introduce ourselves. Not many people know that business cards actually originated centuries before we started to use them for business and intro-ductions. Some sources indicate that business cards origi-nated in China in the fifteenth century.

In the seventeenth century, visiting cards came into regular use. Typically, a messenger from an aristocratic family would present the cards to the servants of the family they were visiting to announce their arrival.

During the time of King Louis XIV, many different rit-uals arose for presenting a visiting card. Just like every-thing else during the reign of the Sun King, visiting cards were extremely glamorous, and the rules were very sophis-ticated. Some even had beautifully engraved ornaments and elegant coats of arms which presented the owner in all his glory. In the nineteenth century, every upper- or mid-dle-class lady and gentleman had to have them.

Modern-day business cards

Today our business cards are part of both our image and our brand. There are a few very basic rules we need to follow when it comes to business cards; if they aren't used well, that first impression can quickly turn into an unfavor-able one.

Your business card should always be crisp and clean, and it's preferable to have a special business card holder to keep your cards neat and tidy. If you're in a foreign coun-try, it's advisable to carry business cards that are translated into the language of the area as well as in your own language. For example, if you're traveling from the U.S. to the United Arab Emirates, it is advised to translate your business card on one side into Arabic (the official language in the country). This gives a great first impression and, because Arab cultures build their business relationships on a personal level first, this can definitely help to secure your future acceptance by Arab businessmen.

Another example: South Africa has twelve official languages, so if you're visiting there, you could easily be confused about which language to translate into. In this instance, it's preferable to keep your business card in English—everyone speaks English in that country. If you would like to create a great first impression, though, it would be priceless to learn a few words in Zulu or Afrikaans before you attend a networking event, so you would need to do your research regarding who would be attending as well.

> **" *Success is where preparation and opportunity meet.* "**
>
> —Bobby Unser

Always keep your business card updated. There is nothing more annoying than a message that your website isn't updated yet or the telephone number on the card is out of service. If you do change your website, domain name, last name, or phone number, be sure to update it immediately and throw away your old cards. It's incredibly unprofessional to make changes at the moment of the event or at the physical card exchange. If you can't take care of your business card, how will you take care of any business relationships? At least that's the image you will portray.

The text in the body of the card needs to be in a readable format. Remember that the point of the business card is to introduce you, so your most important information needs to be readable. Don't use a fancy font which may be difficult to read. Always proofread the text on your business card. A business card doesn't contain many words, but if one or two of those are misspelled, it will be very damaging to your presentation.

It's not mandatory for your business card to be on glossy or expensive paper. Not everyone has a budget for them, but if you follow the guidance above, you'll be just as successful.

Presenting your business card at a networking event

This is a crucial element while networking. When you meet people at a networking event and want to make a connection, you present your business card. Make sure you always carry plenty of your cards to a networking event. In general, it's a good idea to have them with you all the time, even if you're not going to an event.

Don't force yourself on anyone, and always give only one business card to an individual. Don't ever give your business card without having been introduced or asked for it. Don't leave a person with several of your business cards unless they ask for them.

Try to start conversations with people at the event. If you make connections you'd like to follow up on, ask for their business card and if you could give them your card. Ask for a card from every person involved in the conversation—it doesn't really matter if they might be useful to your business or not; it's polite to show interest in every person's business. It's good to be selective, but many times you never know which connection might be productive later on. Besides, it's rude to exclude someone just because they might not be beneficial to your business.

It's always better to collect two business cards and build great connections than to collect two hundred and have nothing come out of any of the connections. The general rule is: if you would like to connect with someone, ask them for their information because you'd like to be in charge of the situation.

If you're given the opportunity to advertise your business with your business card (for example, there's a raffle, or free products are being given away and they ask everyone to leave their cards in a basket), by all means take advantage of the opportunity.

Enjoy the networking process!

CHAPTER TEN

Conflict in Business Situations

It doesn't matter how mature and well-rounded we are, there are times when we will face conflict at work or in business. Sometimes conflict is necessary to wake up our "inner warrior"—the business achiever—or to give us a fresh perspective on where we stand at the present moment. I personally think conflict has positive aspects, because people can learn from their differences. As a matter of fact, conflict can become a booster, unveiling different horizons in your professional or personal life. Here are five main ways to handle conflict from a business etiquette perspective:

Avoid it

Conflict can often be avoided; we might feel that we are compromising ourselves, but, depending on the situation, our maturity can actually be persuasive as a smart business move. Some businesspeople might even test you to see how you react in a steamy business situation; based on the appropriateness of your reaction, you might gain a new client. At the same time, some serious issues simply don't go away. If conflict must be faced, then you should face it with confidence and integrity.

Accommodate it

Here, both parties realize there are differences, but they understand that the main point is to find out whether they can work with those differences: "maybe we can meet each other in the middle."

Compromise

It's important to remember that we all have different perspectives and tolerance for conflict. In the long run, sometimes it's best to compromise and just "let go" of simple situations, as long as it doesn't change our perspective as business professionals and doesn't negatively affect our moral values.

Compete

Competition is everywhere, even if many of us believe that there's a place under the sun for all of us business owners. Competition can be dangerous at times, particularly because some businesses adopt aggressive techniques that can demoralize people who are trying to be creative. At the same time, not many people would like to work with aggressive business professionals who are willing to do anything just to get more business. Highly competitive people usually can't work well with other professionals, for the simple reason that they like to be "the only one."

Collaborate

This is one of the healthiest ways to deal with conflict issues: find a way to work together. There are no two people with the exact same ideas, energy, or creativity. We *can't* be the same, even if we're in the same industry. We all have wonderfully different, unique ways of expressing ourselves, connecting with people, and building our businesses.

My question for you today is: what is *your* model for handling conflict, and why does it work (or not work) for you?

"It doesn't matter where we are coming from, it matters where we are going to ..."

– Maryanne Parker

About the Author

Maryanne Parker, founder of Manor of Manners, a company that specializes in International Etiquette and Protocol training for children and adults based in San Diego, CA.

Poise, elegance, and sophistication were essential to Maryanne's successful years of corporate experiences in Europe, Africa and Northern America. Her unstoppable drive has earned her a Bachelor's degree in Accounting and Financial control from the International University of Economics in Sofia, Bulgaria, world-class experiences, multiple certifications and membership into the Society of Certified Etiquette Trainers in the US.

Maryanne holds an Executive Diploma from the European leading academic institution - International School of Protocol and Diplomacy in Brussels, specializing in diplomacy, protocol, and intercultural relations.

She teaches her two children and clients to model compassion, grace, and respect.

Her methods are learned quickly by her students giving them confidence, skills, self awareness, and knowledge that with manners the American Dream is still possible for anyone.

In her free time, Maryanne Parker is involved with Professional Women Group of Dress for Success, San Diego, which helps underprivileged women to gain financial independence and self sufficiency in their own journey. Here she inspires other women with the message that you don't need money to have class and share etiquette tips on style, dressing for job interviews, and more...

Made in the USA
San Bernardino, CA
02 May 2017